A Lifetime of
RHYMED THOUGHTS

By,
Julia Edwards Pratt

Dedicated to the ones I love;
My amazing parents and 11 siblings
and my 10 loving and beloved children and their children
(currently we have 33 grandchildren),
and not last and never least,
my wonderful husband, Emron Pratt...
Also, my students, neighbors, walking partners,
friends around the world, people who have helped me and those
I've been able to help. I've been blessed with so much love in my
life and often it gushes out into
Rhymed Thoughts.

How this began...

I won the Arboretum poetry contest in Short Hills, New Jersey in 1967 when I was in the 5th grade. Since then I've been writing and rhyming and painting pictures and feelings with words for over half a century. This collection couldn't possibly contain every valentine, or birthday limerick or long ballad about a person or an event that I've written, but it does share many of my thoughts over a lifetime.

–Julia

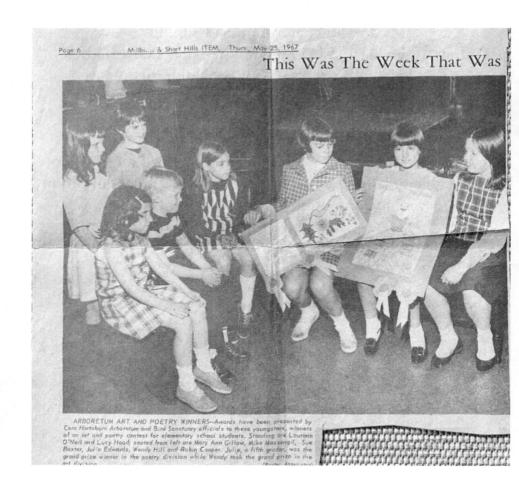

This Was The Week That Was

ARBORETUM ART AND POETRY WINNERS--Awards have been presented by Cora Hartshorn Arboretum and Bird Sanctuary officials to these youngsters, winners of an art and poetry contest for elementary school students. Standing are Laurann O'Neil and Lucy Hood; seated from left are Mary Ann Gitlow, Mike Massengil, Sue Baxter, Julie Edwards, Wendy Hill and Robin Cooper. Julie, a fifth grader, was the grand prize winner in the poetry division while Wendy took the grand prize in the art division.

Who Takes Care of the Dandelions?

Dandelions are beautiful,
Although they are a weed;
They are the fluffiest flower
To ever grow from a seed.

But who takes care of the Dandelions?
Do you wonder who takes care?
I'll tell you the story
Of who put them there.

It was the Dandelion fairy
And her little pet,
The Dandelion lion.
You've heard of him, I bet.

In the springtime of the year,
The little lion came
To protect the little flowers
In his yellow golden mane.

Then a little later
The flowers become white;
Then the little fairy comes
Dancing in delight.

Then, the next thing that they do
They all go to sleep,
Dreaming what will happen,
Safe and warm they keep.

They sleep all through winter
Through snow and showers;
Then they wake up to spring
And dance among the flowers.

By Julia Edwards
Grand Prize winner for poetry--
Arboretum Art and Poetry Contest-
May 25, 1967-

Thoughts about nature...

Robin 17 February 1992

A BEDTIME STORY

Today is a simply marvelous day,
And there's so much to do.
The sun is shining, the birds sing sweet,
The sky is horizon blue.

I know what to do – I'll go for a walk
And see what there is to see.
I'm so excited it's hard to wait.
Why don't you come with me!

Oh, look over there at the flowers fair,
Purple ones, pink and red,
Yellow, orange, blue and white.
It looks like a rainbow bed.

Now bend down close and smell them all.
No fragrance can ever compare.
It is the most beautiful perfume
That Mother Nature could wear.

Look at the bees working so hard.
Their buzzing sounds like a song.
We really should not bother them.
We better hurry along.

There are boys and girls just my age
Playing at the park ahead.
Rather than going home just now
I'll go see my friends instead.

Slides, ladders and merry-go-rounds,
Hanging bars-- EVERYTHING!
My very favorite toy of all
Is the red and white-striped swing.

"Goodbye dear friends, I have to go,"
And into the woods I tramp.
Down the path to a big tall oak
And up the tree I scamp.

Lakes, mountains and endless fields
I'm taller than anyone.
It's been such a simply marvelous day
And we've had lots of fun.

I'm back in my room and my book is closed;
Although my walk seemed quite real,
The things I saw were make believe
And now to my bed I kneel.

I thank my Heavenly Father
For birds that chirp and squawk,
For beaming sun, flowers and trees
For being able to walk.

I climb into my bed so soft
And out of my window I peep,
I say Goodnight to the twinkling stars
Then quickly fall asleep.

By,
Julia Edwards (1973)
I wrote this poem in High School and made it into a little book illustrated
by my younger siblings.

THE ROSE

If you doubt there is a God, look deep into a rose.
See the velvet petals from the folded bud unclosed.
Note the tint and texture and the lovely coloring.
Could blind Nature of itself evolve so fair a thing?
Feel the softness of the petal, breathe the fragrant scent.
Need you waste another thought or further argument?
Here is proof of a creator: God made manifest;
In this little rose we see divinity expressed.

GIFT OF LOVE

Perfect softness, splendor—
The rose in pure array.
A fragrant sweet remember
That gently sparks the day.

Warmth on waking bud
And hidden color glows.
Moisture, soil, mud
And silence, as it grows.

Satin twists and swells.
Each petal forms its soul—
Energy that yells
As beauty wakes in full.

The seedling of a rose
Once planted from above
By Him whose glory shows
In this small gift of love.

By Julia Edwards (I wrote these sometime in college 1974-77)

DAYBREAK

The quiet wakening
of the dawn.
The crispness, the stillness
of day turning on.
The sun reaching in
with a fingering light.
And lingering still
in the denseness of night,
a hushed final scurry
of nocturnal friends.
The changing takes place
and all silence ends.
Sweet music bursts
With a chirrup and whistle,
a coo and a caw
and a tweet in the thistle.
Then soon wake the puppies,
the squirrels and bees.
They wake to the symphony
in the trees.
But few hear the concert,
though tickets are free.
Just feathered musicians
and joggers like me.

Julia Edwards Pratt

(I wrote this in the early 1980's (after a jog) while living in
Tuckahoe, New York. I loved my early morning jogs! It was the only
time I could exercise before the babies woke up and Emron headed
for the train to Manhattan)

THE MYSTERIES OF SILENCE

Silence.
Silence is a triumphal ringing
LOUD as a sound itself.

Replete Silence
renders a holiday
to the mind —
that, freed of listening,
EXPLODES
into the new and unexplored.

Play with the Magic of Silence.
Investigate its POWER...

Climb to the tops of the mountains
and take of the still, unspoiled
silence.

Lie under the cloak of night as the
chips of heaven glitter above you in
silence.

Crawl into the privacy of stillness
found behind the locked door of a familiar room.
Shhhh.

And in the GLORY of SILENCE
Embrace the explosion of
a fresh idea, an original creation, a new experience.
And if you listen to the silence
you may hear the Spirit,
with power enough
to remain ringing in your mind
through the eternities.

Julia Edwards (1974-75) with grateful editing by her mother Jaroldeen Edwards

Machu Picchu

Rays of light
Gently waking
Flower making
Warmly baking
An ancient city.

Rugged mountains
Silhouetting,
Jutting, jetting,
Still protecting
A hidden city.

Vegetation
Green and growing
Ever approaching
Slowly encroaching
A beautiful city.

Misty Clouds
Haunting, floating,
Billowing, bloating,
Hovering, coating
A mysterious city.

Inhabitants
Llamas grazing,
Parrots blazing,
Tourists praising,
The sanctuary city.

By Julia Edwards Pratt--(Thoughts written at 7am on Machu Picchu
while waiting for family to hike down from the Sun Gate, Nov. 2019)

Montezuma Canyon at Night

Look up, look up, look up at the stars!
Can you find Jupiter, Venus or Mars?
The Big Dipper ladle? the belt of Orion?
Scorpion, Bear or Leo the lion?

A star always twinkles and gives you a wink.
A planet stares back like a beacon. They link...
us to past and to present, for light years ago
the rays were released to make galaxies glow.

Polaris guided the Vikings at sea.
The Mayans were experts in astronomy.
It's Abraham's sky, and the Wise Men of old.
The Ancients gazed up and prophets foretold...
of a new star appearing with wonder and awe
for those who looked up and actually saw.

Maybe we need to peer up in the night,
searching the heavens for meaning and light.
What's up there for me? What's up there for you?

Look past the pictures the ancient Greeks drew.

Bask in the glory and diamonds of heaven!

They'll fill you with love and lift you like leaven.

From man-made artificial light- get away!

Drink in the splendor, the vast Milky Way.

Look up, look up, look up, find your star-

A message from Father, who's not very far.

By Julia Edwards Pratt

(inspired by Pete Rossi, 11 June 2020, while stargazing at our farm in Montezuma Canyon)

BUILD MORE SAND CASTLES
(inspired by the poem "I'd Pick more Daisies" By Nadine Stair)

If I could live my life again:

I'd jump more fences
Climb more trees
Cuddle more babies
And sail more seas.
I'd ride more motorcycles
Bounce more balls
Stare at more sunsets
Yodel more calls.
I'd slurp more ice cream
On hot afternoons,
Break more wishbones,
Whistle more tunes.
I'd fail more tests
Tickle more toes
Take more showers
with the garden hose.
I'd pop more balloons
Dance on more tables
Eat more hors d'oeuvres
Fantasize more fables.
I'd hop more hopscotch
Travel more miles
Finger paint more
Share more smiles.
I'd whisper more secrets
Phone more pranks
Color more rainbows
Express more thanks.
I'd go IN more exits
Wear more hats

Do more DON'TS
And pet more cats
I'd giggle more nonsense
Roll through more hay
Blow more dandelions
Make time for more play.
I'd meet more strangers
Roll down hills
Pick more daisies
Eat more candy pills.
I'd sing in more rain
Catch more butterflies
Kick more cans
And throw more pies.

If I could live my life again.
I'd Build More Sand Castles!

Burying Grandma Pratt at Huntington Beach

By Julia Edwards

I wrote this in my teenage years after reading the poem "I'd pick more Daisies" by Nadine Stair. I recommend everyone write their own version. It's fun to think about what you wish you would do more of.

Lake Arrowhead

The evergreen trees grew tall and strong.

The snakelike road kept winding along.

The clear mountain lake invited a throng.

The beautiful day inspired a song.

By, Julia Edwards Pratt

– July 1992– Inspired by a day at the Lake

Sitting, Listening, Thinking

Just sitting, listening, thinking.

Sitting with splendor splashing and swirling down a crystal stream.
Sitting on colorful, jagged, uncomfortable rocks. (which I ignore)
Sitting in a celestial coliseum, canyoned in years of green history.
Sitting with the breeze and the sunbeams playing on my cheeks.

Listening to drops dash and trickle on route to the mother lake.
Listening to the pleasant, sour buzz of a mountain resident.
Listening to pure fun from friends who thrill in loveliness.
Listening to sounds and more, that only I am hearing.

Thinking of everything special to me,
meshed into one thought, one feeling—
love.
Thinking out of my present and into a future beginning,
surrounded by Heavenly Father's magic.

Just sitting, listening, thinking.
That's all.

By Julia Edwards
(Written on a college camping trip with friends
and just taking in the beauty of the moment. - 1975)

Thoughts about Motherhood...

Jeanette with Baby Baylor

NEWBORN

Baby
cradling, caressing
soft, warm, smooth
As I brush my cheek against yours, I feel
Rose Petal.

Baby
kissing, nibbling
sweet, moist, irresistible
As you place fingers in my mouth, I taste
Ambrosia.

Baby
bathing, dressing
clean, fragrant, overpowering
As I hold you close, I smell
Perfume.

Baby
sleeping, smiling
peaceful, beautiful, perfect
As you lay in my arms, I see
Angel

Woman
humming, weeping
grateful, joyful, overcome
Learning of love with her senses
Mother.

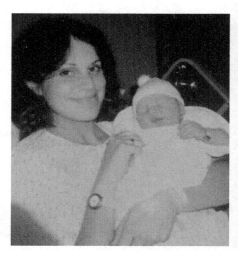

Weston born 29 May 1984

Julia Edwards Pratt
I don't think I was prepared for the overpowering emotions that came with becoming a mother. I really adored my babies. My first child, "Little Emron" was born 29 July 1978.

WHO IS IT?

Who's "cute as a button" without any hair?
As cuddly as "Teddy," but isn't a bear?
A plump "Butterball" that never needs basting,
Yet yummy with kisses, we often are tasting.
"Dumpling," "Pure Sugar," and "Punkin' Pie,"
These at a store you cannot buy.
"Tiger" and "Scooter" and "Wiggly" and "Bumpy,"
Thank goodness they're sturdy and seldom grumpy.
With names like "Bubba" and "Champ" and "Bruiser"
No wonder as parents we come out the loser.
For "Doll face" and "Sweetie" and "Grandma's Heart"
Have become an irreplaceable part;
A "Lil' Cherub" with a heavenly source.
Who is the "Angel"?
A baby of course!

Lauren, born 25 November 1982

Who are You, Little Man?

Your steps are unsure
Your future's a blur
Your words understood
Only by me.

Your actions so limited—
Potential so limitless!
My little man,
Who will you be?

"Little emron" born 29 July

You are but a seed,
planted in a fertile home
with warm love,
and sunny laughter,
and prayerful tears
of caring and understanding.
You will sprout, unfold and
reach upward.
Roots burrowing deep in truth,
Branches stretching to the light,
You will blossom.

But seeing you now—
Seeds all look so similar.
What kind of man
will you
grow up to be?

Julia Edwards Pratt
Just wondering about the potential and future of my little men.

A CRY OF JOY

The congregation files in
With reverence, to their seats.
The chosen hymn is sung by all
Before the Bishop speaks.
The Sacrament is blessed and passed
All's quiet, not a sound.
Then suddenly from in the back
A jolting noise abounds.
An infant's scream bellows strong
His parents claim defeat.
For me, the babe's angelic songs
Help make the spirit sweet.

Julia Edwards

I wrote this before I had children, but I hope that other people feel this way, because I sure had to leave the chapel often with crying babies over the years!

Foster born 9 Jan 1990

A Child's Prayer

Are you real?
Are you there?
Can you really hear my prayer?
Are you real?
Are you near?
Did you hear about my fear?
Do you watch me
as I play?
Do you love me
every day?
Mommy said
your love is true.
That I can really
trust in you.
(That helping us is what you do.)
That YOU love me
more than SHE!
How can that be?
But then you must,
You gave her to me
And Daddy too,
and all the rest
That make my home
the very best.
Are you real?
Yes, I feel
Mommy's faith
When we kneel.

BY Julia Edwards Pratt

DREAMS

Long ago my sleep-filled nights
were full of realistic sights
of me just sailing through the sky
and watching all the world go by.
Asleep, so peaceful and serene,
then, suddenly, a frightful scene
of falling, downward, very near
and waking with a pounding fear—
A trembling darkness all close by
with silent echoes from my cry.
And then, soft step, kind hand, warm glow
brings me to the home I know.
A tender kiss and tucked in tight,
I'm launched into my dream-filled flight.

And now, with sleepless nights, I dream
of children waking with a scream.
I sail into the room of fear
and hold the frightened child near.
A sleepy peace soon fills the room
and scares away nocturnal gloom.
Then back to bed my dream I keep,
wondering as I drift in sleep
about my realistic flights
to comfort in the care-filled nights.

Julia Edwards Pratt

Comforting a frightened child in the middle of the night is one of those important parental tasks, but sometimes I wondered if it really happened.

MOMMY'S HAIR

(Did you ever have a toddler obsessed with hair? I did)

Oh, how I love my Mommy's hair,
My Mommy's soft and golden hair.
I love to find it everywhere.
It's so easy.

Clinging to my socks I find
A hair or two, but I don't mind.
The baby's fingers are entwined.
It's so funny.

I twist it round my finger tight,
Or stretch and break it with my might,
Or hold it up against the light.
It's so nice.

I find her brush, each hair I tug
And watch them drift down to the rug.
And when she sees, I get no hug.
It's worth it.

Once, into her room I stepped
and up upon her pillow crept
Just to smell where her hair slept.
It's so sweet.

Oh, how I love my Mommy's hair,
My Mommy's soft and golden hair.
I love to find it everywhere.
It reminds me of her.

Julia Pratt

A TEACHING MOMENT

My child and I are alone,
isolated from a crowded world
by a special moment,
brief and unplanned.
Joining hands and hearts,
words and thoughts
we learn.

My child learns about :
Nature- "How did a bird build that nest?"
Or
Feelings- "Why am I sad?"
Or
God- "Where did the new baby come from?"

And I relearn
what an honor it is to be a mother.

Christian 11 December 1987

A KINDERGARTEN KISS

The schoolyard is alive again
(A nervous smile, a kiss).
My son begins his school crusade
And I already miss
The years of baby, toddler, child.
I wipe away my tear
That's blended with his lingering kiss.
The memories seem so clear.

I recall that first, wet kiss
When my son was one.
Since birth, I'd smothered him with love,
So he tried one for fun.
He opened up his mouth so wide
As if to take a bite.
He licked my cheek, then smiled to see
If he did it right.

At two, it was a muddy kiss.
Dirt was his favorite treat.
At three, it was a sticky kiss
To thank me for a sweet.
Then, at four, lipstick smears
Brought my cheek wet joy.
Playing with Mommy's makeup
Was then the favorite toy.

Now at five, so grown up,
This moment marks an end
Of spending days together.
I'll miss my constant friend.

Julia Edwards Pratt
(when my first child went to Kindergarten- 1983)

Kite Strings

My daughter Elizabeth came home from Kindergarten with a well-known poem, "Children are Like Kites." By Erma Bombeck. It was in the shape of a kite and sent to help worried parents let go. The poem ended with these words; "and somehow you know that it won't be long before that beautiful creature will snap the lifeline that bound you together and soar as it was meant to soar free and alone." Wait a minute! Although I think a kite is a great metaphor for children—if a kite string snaps the kite comes crashing down. So, I rewrote the ending.
Here's the new poem.

Children
are like kites.
You spend a lifetime
trying to get them off the
ground. You run with them until
you are breathless – they crash –
you add a longer tail – they hit the rooftop.
You pluck them out of the spout, you patch and
comfort, adjust and teach. You watch them lifted by the
wind and assure them that someday they'll fly! Finally
they are airborne, but they need more string and
you keep letting it out, and with each twist of
the ball of twine, there is a sadness that goes
with the joy, because the kite becomes
more distant, and somehow you
know that it won't be long
before that beautiful creature
will fly and soar out of your
sight. But remember you
must never let go
for if you do the
kite will fall.
The lifeline
is love.

By Erma and Me

Elizabeth- 1st day of Kindergarten,

Reflections of a Mother and Her Teenage Daughter

We look in the mirror.
You ask, "Is this outfit alright?"
"Is it too tight?"
Suddenly I see
a shadow of me
two decades ago.

Is it your asking eyes,
your pinched brow,
or the way you stand?
I don't quite know.
But in you, I catch a glimpse
of the forgotten me.

We would have been best friends!
I'd never have to say
"No, you can't wear that"
"Clean your room"
"Get off the phone!"

We would have talked for hours
and shared our secrets,
And I would have kept those
secrets a secret...
And I will now
if you give me a chance.

We would have "hung out" together
for we enjoy the same things,
some of which I can't do now—
But if you invite me
we can still have fun.

We would have laughed together.
            And you know,
                        we need to do more laughing.
Sometimes it all gets too serious.

We are not identical.
            Our differences would have offered
                        variety and interest.
Let's not let our differences
            divide us now.

Because in two decades or so
            you'll stand at the mirror
                        with <u>your</u> daughter...
And her outfit will be too tight.
            And you'll hope she understands
                        And knows that you love her.

And then you'll call your best friend
            for advice-
                        And it will be me.

By Julia Edwards Pratt (about 1996)

My girls

MOTHER WITH A FULL QUIVER; A RARE SPECIES

A mother with a quiver that is full
is an extraordinary animal.
Her talents are unique.
She's sort of an antique.
Her life is simply everything but dull!

This kind of mother is part stork, I fear.
She has a baby every other year.
Her children seem so endless,
but, never are they friendless.
Her home does overflow with love and cheer.

Like a squirrel, she instinctively does hoard
tons of food that is not easy to afford.
You'll see her at the store
with two carts full, maybe more.
Never get behind her – take my word.

Like a work horse, this mother's never lazy.
Her toddler riding Momback calls her "Daisy."
She takes teens near and far
with horsepower from the car.
It would drive another human being crazy.

Just like a cat, she prowls and she lurks.
Seeking bargains is a job she never shirks.
She's cunning and she's shrewd.
But she's never ever rude.
Saving money, spending wisely's how she works.

Like an opossum, her happy babies cling
To her back, around her neck they will swing.
But they never slow her down
as she runs throughout the town.
It is quite a remarkable thing.

An owl with the wisdom of the sages
for children with the spectrum of all ages
Is definitely a must!
This mother's always just
and rarely flares up in angry rages.

Some say that with the unicorn she links.
But, this mother's far from being extinct.
Although her number's dwindled,
her love of life is kindled.
A love that will pass down through hearts, I think.

My quiver! Emron, Jeanette, Nadine, Lauren, Weston, Parker,
Christian, Foster, Robin, Elizabeth

THE FINISHED STORY

The children all gathered round Mother's warm knees.
Looking tenderly into their eyes,
She saw eager faces, easy to please
Waiting anxiously for their surprise.

"Tonight I will give you a gift so dear—
One you won't want to forget.
So listen with care and draw up near."
William yelled, "It's a story I bet!"

"The story about Prince Charming?" asked Robin.
Malcolm added, "a cowboy or two?"
Weston wished for a ghost story filled with suspense.
"No", Mother said, "Something new!"

The children instinctively settled right down.
They felt a warm surge of love
Cradling their hearts in a blanket of care-
was a hush and a peace from above.

"I'll tell you a story about a great man
Who loves you more than you know.
He lived, prayed, suffered and died
To help you righteously grow."

Mother with tears in her eyes, couldn't speak.
The children could not understand,
'Til suddenly, enveloped by love, they knew
It was Jesus, the Great I Am!

After moments passed of peaceful silence,
She began her story of old,
But Mother looked into her children's sweet eyes
And knew that her story'd been told.

My mother was an amazing storyteller and was a woman of strong faith. I wrote
this in high school about her, to thank her for teaching me to know about and
love Jesus Christ. 1974 Julia Edwards

MOVIN' OUT

My arms outstretched,
Please take my hand.
Through years of trials,
Now, I understand.
I've not much time.
The moments are few
To tell you, Mother
How much I love you.

My life has new paths
That beckon me
And what's ahead
I cannot see.
I'll keep the memories
Of yesterday
Today can't hold me;
I'm on my way.

Speak to me softly
Let's strengthen our ties
I see tomorrow
Shining in your eyes.
You're in my heart
For now, and always.
I love you Mother.
Thank you for my yesterdays.

Julia Edwards (Graduated from Scarsdale HS 1974)

These were new lyrics I wrote to a song called "Movin' On." We sang it for
Mother's Day

PEARLS

Birthdays after fifty,
I'd sooner skip.
Still, I opened up the gift.
A strand of pearls
from grown children
now scattered.
Each gem
not quite white
not quite round
yet, perfect in its own way.

I remember
long ago pearls
pulled from my neck
by innocent young hands.
The strand broke.
Beads slipped away
and scattered.

Life seemed endless then.
My home, a family portrait,
with everyone present.

Only an illusion.

My firstborn grown,
left home.
Then, as if my strand of pearls
was cut,
one by one
my children
slipped away
and scattered.
I miss my young pearls.

Julia E. Pratt

MY PERSONAL HISTORY

My media mind is full of memories.
My cerebrum stores vaults of little videos
to warm the heart
or tickle the funny bone.
Your little faces, every detail,
are so precious to me.

But the images are fading.

I want to restore and preserve my archives.
I want to share my treasures with you, my children,
before a feeble mind locks the door
and loses the key.

No camera can retake the fading photos.
No DVD can dub my mental movies.

And so I must write.
It is hard, and sometimes painful.

It is the script of my life.
It is your inheritance.
It is love.

I love you with all my heart,
MOM

Julia Edwards Pratt
(Recent – In fact, this collection is part of that personal history)

Thoughts about
Specific Individuals...

My seminary class 2000 - Flower Mound TX

Happy Birthday Mother
February 23, 1989

I searched within the Hallmark aisle
To find the perfect card.
To spot one that conveyed my thoughts
Was surprisingly hard.
The cards all said "I love you"
(But you already know that.)
With pictures of hearts and flowers
And children and even a cat.
Some said "Thank you" for my life,
my memories and childhood too.
But none of them completely shared
My feelings about you.
And so, in simple verse I'll try
To share my feelings here.
But it's much tougher than I thought
To make my message clear.
There are no words that can express
My love strongly enough.
And I cannot find the words
To thank you deeply enough
For unconditional love you've given,
Your example of service and cheer.
There are no words to wish you enough
Joy in the coming year.
I hope this poem will absorb
The feelings of my heart,
So you can FEEL abiding love
Even when apart.

Julia Edwards Pratt

Anything I did right as a mother was because of my mother, Jaroldeen
Asplund Edwards. Words still cannot express how much I loved her and
how incredible she was.

Weston Eyring Edwards

Brilliant yet wise
Strong yet gentle
Successful yet honest
Admired yet humble
Independent yet prayerful
Righteous yet tolerant
Serious yet playful
Exuberant yet reverent
Wealthy yet giving
Diligent yet patient
Direct yet loving
Disappointed yet content
My Father and yet, forever my daddy.

By Julia Edwards Pratt-- May 1991

A Complimentary Couple
By Julia Edwards Pratt

Complimentary colors with opposite hues
Almost clash.
Yet, joined,
They become intertwined.
Inseparable.
Yellow and Purple - Spring Daffodils and Crocuses
Orange and Blue – a Flaming Autumn Sunset
Red and Green – Christmas

A Complimentary couple with opposite hues
Complimented and completed each other.
Clashing conversations sparked,
Igniting an eternal friendship.
Joined in the springtime of youth,
Intertwined through life's sojourn
Until the sunset of life.
Inseparable in Christ.
Weston and Jaroldeen.

Roommates

I live on one long windy path
With obstacles I face
I gladly accept encouraging hands
To help me quicken my pace
I trip over barriers of temptation
But through them I still plod
Hoping that I won't stumble
Away from the iron rod.

I'll strive for all that's good and true
Until my journey ends
If I need help, I'll turn to you
My dearest, closest friends.

My Walking Partner

We walk and talk and walk and talk
       and walk and talk around the block.

Two miles round, three days a week
       for five years now we've met to speak
       and share the details of our lives.

It only looks like exercise.

For all those steps that we can claim,
       our figures look about the same.

Although the walk gives us a lift
       it's from the talk, we benefit.

We talk of all that comes to mind—
       news, recipes, sales we find,
       schools, homes, our neighborhood.

Mostly, we talk of Motherhood.
       How to handle a temper or fight.
How to help them read and write.
       She's walked me through three pregnancies
With three boys, she's had emergencies!
       (broken bones and bloody knees)

In ways we're different, she and I
But love for children binds the tie.

The alarm goes off at five forty-five.
The darkness of morning is barely alive.
At times we're not really awake 'til we meet
        which is nearly a quarter-mile down the street.

But then the sharing begins to take place.
And new ideas help problems erase.
A friendship and caring fills the space
The new day we are ready to face.

By Julia Edwards Pratt-
inspired by Kitty Tibbets my walking partner 1986-1997
and with special love and gratitude to all my walking partners over
the years; Nancy, Paula, Marianne, Jan, Jean, Marty, Janice et al.

Kitty

BOOTS

He was the pick of the litter
A beauty of white and black
One of the Pace's puppies
Soon to be in our pack.

He was so cute and cuddly
And grew to be so HUGE.
People doubt his pedigree
But we have the papers as proof.

A border collie purebred
With a coat as thick as a bear
And a soul as kind as a kitten
A gentleness that's rare.

As a young male he had SPIRIT.
His strength and drive could knock
You off your feet or lose the leash
And drag you round the block.

Boots was marking EVERYTHING.
We gave up hopes of breeding.
His solitary purpose then–
to love and do our bidding.

He was smart and handsome
Loyal, true and sweet.
Whenever you returned
He'd be right there to greet.

A good jogging companion
A fun frisbee golf buddy
A fellow explorer,
Not afraid to get muddy.

Boots and Cal together-
Cal massaging with his claws
And who can forget the image—
Boot's massaging with his jaws.

Grandchildren loved and played
With Boots — all big and burly
Even with babies he
Was completely trustworthy.

Each person in our family,
Had a Boots connection
The joy and guilt of pets
Causes a deep reflection.

Boots was a special dog.
We're sure he's up in heaven
And we hope we'll be blessed
To take care of Him again.

A Special tribute and thanks to all our pets; bunnies, cats,
chickens, ducks, rats, hamsters, fish, turtles, birds, frogs…
But especially to our two faithful dogs, Honey and Boots.

JEANETTE
R e s u m e

Jeanette's the best at everything
She puts her heart into.
She tackles like a linebacker
And pushes til she's through.
No mountain is too big to climb,
No river she can't cross.
She works well when she's on a team.
She's also a great boss.
Like Rachel Ray she's quite a chef.
Her food both looks and tastes good.
Maneuvering her giant truck
She knows the neighborhood.
Her home décor impresses all.
She has the Midas touch—
A confident artistic eye,
That's rare and needed much.
She's smart with a computer.
She's clever with a phrase.
She balances her numbers;
Her bills she always pays.
Her voice is like an angel.
(She's better than Celine.)
Her body's like a model.
She's beautiful and lean.
A college degree from BYU,
A mother of six kids,
An honest and hardworking gal—
Now who will start the bids?
She's organized and loving.
She's really like no other.
These skills and more she's honed
While being a full-time mother.
She's really quite magnificent
I'm telling you the truth.
And she's highly OVER qualified
For whatever you need her to do!

After raising six children as a full-time mother, Jeanette started looking into the job market. She called me one day discouraged because she didn't have much "experience." I wrote her this resume, just to let her know how amazing and talented and marketable I think she is.

EARLY MORNING SEMINARY

Reaching in the dark to shut off the beeping in my dreams,
wishing it was a dream.

Fumbling in the shadows for clothing that matches
so I don't cause a scene.

Riding through streets of black and night,
that rock me back to sleep.

Walking in a fog through the fog to the door,
emerging from the deep...

Into the light, I squint until my eyes adjust,
it's almost too bright.

Into the light, as I learn of the Savior,
The Lord becomes my light..

Into the light, as scriptures ignite my mind,
truth becomes clear.

Into the light, where testimonies are shared,
faith extinguishes fear.

Into the light, as friendships are kindled,
I'm not afraid to smile.

Into the light, the Spirit warms my soul
I hope it stays awhile.

I absorb the light and feel its wakening and
strengthening glow.

Illuminated and ready to shine,
Into the dark I go.

This is dedicated to my 6 years of seminary students. They were amazing.

Thoughts about LOVE...

It all started Valentine's Day 1977.

I had surprised Emron by leaving a pink heart shaped lemon merengue pie in his apartment, but I hadn't gotten any response or reaction. It was 11pm and I had concluded that Emron didn't really like me as much as I thought he did. Then a knock, and he was at the door with a homemade Valentine.

Emron officially proposed the next day! We've been exchanging homemade Valentine's every February 14th ever since, and most of mine have rhymed.

Kindergarten 1961

MY SWEETHEART

As I reflect upon the love
that saturates my heart,
I think of all the dear ones
who each take up a part.
The children that I've borne
each have a special place.
They fill my life up to the brim.
Will I run out of space?
No, I think my heart will grow
as each new child is born.
Yet, it's hard to meet each need.
My heart is often torn.
I hope you never feel squeezed out.
T'would break my heart in two
For you were first – most precious of all.
My heart belongs to you.

Julia Pratt

OUR LOVE

Love is romance so private and dear.
Love is success with a raise every year.
Love is a date when it's just us two.
(alas those dates are far too few.)
Love is graduation, new house and car
Reaching and finding the brightest star.
Love is a baby all healthy and new
The blessing before when it's almost due.
Love is the temple and being sealed.
Love is priesthood and being healed.
But love is also much, much more.
It's diapers and crying and dishes galore.
It's budgets and breakdowns and painting 'til two.
It's gripes and grunts to name a few.
Love is <u>our</u> life, together forever,
And nothing can split us never, ever.

I really do love you!
Feb 14, 1982

It just gets better and better

Dear Emron, I cannot bear
That you not know how much I care.
I think of you when we're apart
You hold a big chunk of my heart.

When I can't call and hear your voice
My day is down, 'til I rejoice
when you come home, for I'm in touch
with you, my love -- love you so much!

You need to know, so I'm writing this letter
That our love just gets better and better.
Now twenty years from our first Valentine
I say once again, "Will you be mine?"

Eternally Yours,
Julia (Valentine's Day 1997)

Valentine's Day 2000

A child of God
A gift from God
A gift to me
A child of mine
A gift of love
A love from God
God is love
I love you,
Child.

1 John 4:8
He that loveth not
knoweth not God,
For God is love."

Mom

(I also write Valentine's to my children every year.)

Nadine 1 June 1981

Love One Another and Serve One Another

How can we Pratts love one another?
From the parents right down to each sister and brother?
Just saying "I love you" is not enough.
Especially when playing gets hurtful and rough.
We need to <u>show</u> each other we care.
We need to give service, be kind and share.
Here are a few of the special ways.
Each person could have happier days.
Parker can use lots of help you know –
–with shoes and clothes and a good nose blow.
Weston needs help on how to play fair,
And how to be happy and how to share.
Lauren loves company when she draws.
She's learning to read and obey family laws.
Nadine needs encouragement to make her own choices.
She needs a home filled with love and sweet voices.
Jeanette needs a family that helps her have fun,
Who lifts her and praises her jobs well done.
Emron needs an interested, listening ear.
He needs friends who are patient and filled with cheer.
Mom and Dad need help with the house that's true.
But we also need friendship from each one of you.
So let's start today to <u>show</u> our love,
By "serving one another" as our Savior above.
By Julia Edwards Pratt – 1986
Family Scripture– Mosiah 4:15
"Teach them to love one another and to serve one another"

LOVE GROWS

Everyone's changing every day.
And we all grow in a different way.
Some get fatter
Some get lighter
Some get dumber
Some get brighter
Some get funnier
Some get taller
Some get wiser
Some get smaller
We may change the way we act
Or change the way we look. In fact,
We can be what we want to be.
That is the gift of agency.

And, however YOU want to grow and change,
Or take your parts and rearrange.
I want you to know that whatever you do,
Whatever you want to grow up to,
That I will always and forever LOVE YOU!!!

And speaking of growing and changing and love,
Our family's being sent a gift from above.
The reason is very clear to my view.
This person wants a (brother/sister) like you!

I love you SO much.
Mom

Valentine's Day 1994- This was the Valentine/ baby announcement to my children for their final sibling, Elizabeth, who was born in August.

NO MATTER WHAT...

No matter what you do
No matter what you say
No matter how close
Or how far away
No matter what you wear
On any given day
Whether you are serious
Or even at play
No matter if you're weird
Or sad and grey
No matter if you're happy
Or if you go astray.
No matter <u>what</u> – I want to relay
That I will be there
And will always pray
That no matter what
You'll be okay.
And I'll love you
To my dying day
(and beyond.)
Mom

Parker 29 December 1985

<u>Kissing</u>

Kissing is special! That's certainly true!
And there's so many kinds that are fun to do!

A kiss on the cheek, a peck on the face,
Says an "I Love You" that's hard to erase.

When leaving for school, when you've done your best,
-kissing tears away after bombing a test.

A kiss at the top of your head means -be good
And do all the things that good children should!

A kiss on each eye helps close them up tight
As you're tucked into bed to dream through the night.

An Eskimo kiss on the nose means we're chilly,
Or we missed our aim, or we're just being silly.

A flying kiss can go anywhere!
A kiss and a blow sends our love through the air.

Yes kissing is special, kissing is great
But <u>serious</u> kissing must wait til you date!

Show friends your love in other ways.
But, remember to kiss your mother, ALWAYS!

With lots of love and XXXXXX
Mom * Valentine's Day 1998

TRUE LOVE LOVES

LOVE is a noun, a palpable thing.
Can cause you to cry
Or spark you to sing.

The feelings from LOVE abide in the heart.
At times it o'erflows,
Sometimes tears apart.

Sweeter than chocolate, hotter than fire
Fresher than flowers;
LOVE's our desire.

But candy gets old, the flames can die down,
And roses wilt—
When love's just a noun.

'Cause LOVE is a verb! It's what we must DO
to keep LOVE alive,
and vibrant and new.

The tender touch, the compliment
Just "hanging out"
Is time well spent.

Forgo what you want, to care for another.
Prefer their happiness—
Treasure each other.

The little things begin to mount.
The roses, the chocolate
And candlelight count!

LOVE is a sentence, both parts together
-The subject and predicate-
Make LOVE last forever.

By Julia Edwards Pratt (Happy Valentine's Day 2020)

I LOVE YOU MORE

I love you more than ice cream.

I love you more than candy.

Love you more than my favorite flick.

More than a man who's handy.

I love you more than lentil soup,

Or grapefruit or cranberry juice.

I feel happier when I'm with you,

then when my pants feel loose.

I love you more than vacation trips.

More than wads of money.

I love you more than our own home.

Love you much more than Honey. (our dog)

I love you more than anyone

or anything on earth.

For I'm in you and you're in me-

Our marriage was a birth

to a love and a oneness

that is sealed from on high.

So, I sure hope you love me

more than lemon merengue pie.

Julia Edwards Pratt

Thoughts on Holidays...

For me the Holiday Season is all connected from
November to January. How can I pick a favorite?
Starting with feelings of gratitude on
Thanksgiving, that prepares us for generous giving
at Christmastime—
and with thoughts of the Savior, the New Year
makes me want to change and try to be a little bit
better. I Love it all!

A Thanksgiving POEM

T is for the turkey, a big plump butterball
H is for the hike where some run, some walk, some crawl
A is for our appetites which shrink after dinner.
N is for "No Thanks" if we said it, we'd be thinner!
K is for the kindness the whole family did display
S completes the "thanks" to our parents for the day
G is for great pilgrims who thanked the Lord for land.
I is for the Indians who made the feast so grand
V is for our visitors who make today great too
      (Now add an S to)
I
N
G
      Cause that's what we're going to do!
Sing your favorite Thanksgiving Hymn, *i.e.*

For the beauty of the earth
For the beauty of the skies
For the love which from our birth
Over and around us lies.
Lord of all, to Thee we raise
This our hymn of grateful praise.

WHO HEARD A WHO?

Who would have given
A hoot about Who's.
Or even have hinted
Of being amused
By the Whoville Village
Liking Christmas a lot
And a Grinch who lived North
Who most surely did not!
Well a fellow named Suess,
A hilarious sort,
Put his pencil to work
And began to explort.
He loved little children.
He loved Christmas too
And combined he created
Each loveable Who.
The Grinch that stole Christmas,
A villain to start,
By the end of the story
Had stolen our hearts.
The plot is enchanting
To both young and old.
And on every Christmas
The story's retold.
Thank you dear Suess
For your stories so dear.
For the Who's and the Grinches
We so love to hear.
Yes, Christmas was SAVED
When the Grinch Heard a Who
And if you recall-
"Horton Hears a Who" too
But that is a story
For another day…

Julia Edwards (college)

<u>Hush – It's Christmas!</u>

It might be warm and pleasant and bright
There may be ice or rain in sight.
We may have snow on Christmas night.
In Dallas you just never know.

But oh, we'll see a million lights,
Glittering people and holiday sights.
Parties and music will fill up the nights.
For Christmas here is aglow.

Immersed in the laughter and lively lush
Of presents and candy and hustle and rush,
We'll search for that peaceful, meaningful hush
And tune into spiritual things.

Like wisemen of old we gather our treasure
For giving to loved ones brings joy beyond measure.
And giving to strangers gives deeper pleasure.
We learn that from the kings.

We try to sing carols, like angels, with zeal.
And like the shepherds, we prayerfully kneel.
To help make the long-ago birth seem more real,
The birth of Jesus, the Child.

So turn down the lights and gather around
Let's talk of the babe laid on the straw mound.
This is where Christmas will truly be found
Holy Infant, so tender and mild.

By Julia Edwards Pratt – Dec 1989

The Savior's Birth
A New World Perspective

A few had faith
in shared strength
shared witness and
shared love
for God and His Son.

but still the piercing Fear
of brutal death.

"Now it came to pass that there was a day set
apart by the unbelievers, that all those who
believed in those traditions should be put to
death except the sign should come to pass."

A man in humble bow
shed tears for Heaven's whisper.
Softly, he listened,

"Lift up your head and be of good cheer;
for behold the time is at hand, and on
this night shall the sign be given,
and on the morrow come I into the world."

A day, a night and a day,
light upon light upon light
sun joined with Son,
the Savior of souls.
Souls saved by His birth
and saved by His death,
Filled with pure love.
His love.

"a new star did appear, according to the word." 3 Nephi 1

THINKING AND DREAMING OF CHRISTMAS

When I think of Christmas…
Little **LIGHTS** aglow
Sparkling trees and bright streets
Make a wondrous show
Fire flames and candles
Flicker with delight
I want to stay up very late
To see the Christmas sights.

When I think of Christmas…
GIFTS for everyone
Dolls and trains and puzzles
Balls and games so fun!
Presents wrapped with ribbons,
Secrets out of sight.
I want to stay up very late
And take a peek tonight.

When I think of Christmas
Stockings filled with **TREATS**
Sugar plums and gumdrops
Gingersnaps so sweet
Candied little houses
Homemade chocolates too
I want to stay up very late
And lick and taste and chew.

When I think of Christmas…
MUSIC everywhere!
Bells are softly pealing
Singers in the square
Songs about the stable,
Or Santa's coming soon.
I want to stay up very late
And carol to the moon

When I think of Christmas…
CHILDREN here and there!
Noses pressed to windows
Excitement's in the air.
Time to tell the story
Of a little manger bed
I want to head upstairs tonight
And sleep and dream instead.

For when I dream of Christmas
LIGHTS are twinkling stars
GIFTS are kingly treasures.
Bethlehem's not far.
CANDY is a shepherd's cane.
I see **ANGELS** in the snow.
BABY JESUS sleeping is
The sweetest dream I know.

Julia Edwards Pratt (requested and improved by
George Sloan who turned it into a song) Christmas
2016

New Year's Resolutions 2020

Julia Edwards Pratt

Twenty pounds to lose again

Be a better spouse and friend

Be on time. Read the scriptures

Finally organize the pictures

Eat much less. Read much more.

Like I said the year before.

Resolutions look familiar

Every year the same until your

Wondering if you're simply stuck

With stubborn genes or just bad luck.

Why's my list again the same?

How can I make a permanent change?

Maybe I need a different approach.

Maybe I need a Heavenly Coach!

We're so beset with being slim.

Focus now on following Him.

Who do we love? What do we prize?

Work on our hearts more than our thighs.

What is it we really treasure?

That may be a better measure

Of how we're doing year by year.

Running the treadmill of life, I fear

Makes us restless, beat and bored.

Take the stairs that lead to the Lord!

The race of life at times seems endless

Disappointing, hard and friendless

With His Light, His Word and Grace

We'll run with joy and win the race.

So as we make our list each day

Plan to veer and go His way.

And while we're heading to the gym

Bow our heads and first choose Him.

Thoughts about our Missions...

Mexico City Mexico, Oct 2015 – May 2017

Lima Peru – August 2018 – March 2020

LEAVE TO RECEIVE

Leave the grandkids, hug each one.
Miss their birthdays, miss the fun.

Leave your friends, your comfort zone.
Leave behind all you have known.

Leave your money, there's enough.
Leave your treasures, store your stuff.

Leave your pets, leave your home.
Leave the familiar. Get ready to roam!

Leave the ease of retirement
'Cause if you're willing, you'll be sent

To...

Receive the call to serve the Lord
To shine His light and share His word.

Receive the test to walk by faith
To trust in Him and not in fate.

Receive the dream to live abroad.
Your time's enriched while serving God.

Receive a culture, from the start~
And new friends will lodge in your heart.

Receive a love that's strong and new,
A oneness with your spouse and you.

Receive the chance to use your gifts.
Mentor, train, love and lift.

Receive the trials with humility,
And learn to say, "It's not about me."

Receive and see the miracles flow;
Believing hearts will come to know.

Receive some time to dedicate
To really, fully consecrate.

Yes, leaving is hard, and so is a mission
It takes great faith to make the decision.

But boundless blessings you'll want to achieve
And you have to LEAVE before you RECEIVE.

Julia Edwards Pratt

(2020 - Thinking about the sacrifices and blessings
of serving a full-time senior mission)

Feliz día de San Valentin!!! 2017

My mission to Mexico has taught me *muchas cosas*

Quiero riding *caballos* to see the *mariposas*

Quiero squeezing *limones* all over my *comida.*

Quiero the museos and enjoy a good *corrida.*

Quiero brilliant colors and everywhere *la flor*

Quiero serving the Lord. *Mi jefe es el Señor.*

Quiero working with Emron, my beloved *esposo*

Our *tiempo* together *es muy feliz y gozoso.*

The *otra cosa* I have learned from my *corazón*

Abrazos cannot be replaced by the telephone.

Quiero my familia, more than ever before!

My *hijos* and my *hijas,* I truly do adore.

My *nueras* and my *yernos, quiero lo mismo* too.

Each brings *algo especial, divertido* and new

My *nietos y nietas* are *bonitos y preciosos*

Can´t wait to see y'all and give you lots of *besos*!

Con Amor,   Mom and Grammy

Here is the translation key:

muchas cosas=many things / corazón=heart

amor=love / quiero=I love / abrazos=hugs

besos=kisses / caballos=horses / mariposas=butterflies

limones=limes / comida=food / museos=museums

corrida=tour / flor=flower / lo mismo=the same

algo=something / esposo=spouse

feliz y gozoso=happy and joyful / mi jefe=my boss

el Señor=the Lord / hijos=sons / hijas=daughters

nuera=daughter-in law / yerno=son-in-law

divertido=fun / nietos=grandsons

nietas=granddaughters / bonito=beautiful

preciosos=precious

I dream of a place...   (2016)

I dream of a place
   Where colors explode
   Where splashes and dashes are quaint
   No need to conform;
   Pick your favorite hue—
   Go crazy with buckets of paint.

I dream of a place
   Where blossoms prolific
   adorn every sidewalk and tree.
   Every home has a space
   that's secret and safe
   where flowers grow effortlessly.

I dream of a place
   Where fruit is a-plenty,
   Just like the Garden of old.
   All colors and shapes
   All ripened and sweet
   And on every corner they're sold.

I dream of a place
   Where love's in the air.
   And passerby strangers are kind
   When you walk down the street
   All will smile and greet
   Goodness and warmth you will find.

I dream of this place
I live in a dream.
I live in Mexico.

Me Gusta El Perú

Me gustan Inca Colas
Y Andean bolsas
Me gusta anís
me hace feliz
Me gustan las llamas
Y calientes pijamas
Me gusta comer papa
Y trabajar con papa
Me gustan los cóndores
Y todo tipo de flores
Me gusta la clase de ejercicio
Y la clase del evangelio
Me gustan dulces y flan
Y el Eterno Plan
Machu Picchu es encantador
El ceviche es mejor
Me gusta cantar con el coro
Con cada misionero
Me gusta ají de gallina
Y mi amiga Karina
Me gustan pollos a las brazas
Y besos y abrazos
Pero lo más importante para mi
ES YO AMO A TI!!!!!
Con Amor,
Abuela Grammy
Dia de los enamorados 2019 in Peru
(Still desperately trying to learn Spanish)

Thoughts about Faith...

<u>Nearer to Thee</u>

When I was very small, I can vividly recall
Jesus' picture on the wall
Every Sunday.
His tender loving face, glowed with a tender grace
As He looked up into space
So far away.
I remember well His eyes, so convincing warm and wise
Full of wonderful surprise
And beaming light.
And as I peered from the front row, then, I really didn't know
That someday He would show me
What was right.
That picture always will give me memories that fulfill
And I even love it still
Like no other.
But through many a painful year and many a prayerful tear
He's not a painting near,
He's my brother.

By Julia Edwards (1975- And this is the painting that inspired
this poem)

<u>Testimony</u>

The heart overflows

and filling the eye

warms a smooth cheek

giving birth to a cry.

Julia Edwards

(1976- I can't bear my testimony without weeping. I wrote this in Church as I was experiencing it. I was too emotional to stand and bear my testimony so I wrote this instead.)

AGENCY

My mind resembles an empty book
With pages blank and bare.
And as I diligently look
What I want to know isn't there.

I often wish that God would give
His omniscient thoughts to me,
But I must gain knowledge as I live
My author <u>must</u> be me.

Julia Edwards (another college poem)

UNANSWERED QUESTIONS

Who?
What?
When?
I search
my familiar chamber
of "Whys"
with questions
requiring simple
replies
which hide
as I seek
knowledge...

...so I wait
impatiently...

...and then,
on sore knees,
the silent whisper
of Heaven's release
leaves questions unanswered,
but my heart now
at peace.

Julia Edwards (sometime in college 1974-1977)

THE DOCTRINE AND COVENANTS

Our struggling past,
Persecutions strong.
Reviled against,
The Saints pushed on.

The group was small
But strength in few
And faith in truth
Gave courage, new.

Discouragement
And grief were there.
Nomads forced
To great despair.

With watching hope,
The Lord above
Soothed their needs
With words of Love.

By Julia Edwards

(1976- I wrote this at BYU while taking a Religion
class in Church History)

UNANSWERED QUESTIONS

Who?
What?
When?
I search
my familiar chamber
of "Whys"
with questions
requiring simple
replies
which hide
as I seek
knowledge...

...so I wait
impatiently...

...and then,
on sore knees,
the silent whisper
of Heaven's release
leaves questions unanswered,
but my heart now
at peace.

Julia Edwards (sometime in college 1974-1977)

THE DOCTRINE AND COVENANTS

Our struggling past,
Persecutions strong.
Reviled against,
The Saints pushed on.

The group was small
But strength in few
And faith in truth
Gave courage, new.

Discouragement
And grief were there.
Nomads forced
To great despair.

With watching hope,
The Lord above
Soothed their needs
With words of Love.

By Julia Edwards

(1976- I wrote this at BYU while taking a Religion
class in Church History)

HOPE

There's hope in the rising sun,
waking up the day.
There's hope in the infant Son
laying in the hay.

There's hope in a waterfall,
fresh and clean and clear.
There's hope in "Living Waters",
who cleanses every tear.

There's hope in a "Gathering"
with family breaking bread.
There's hope in the "Bread of Life"
who keeps our spirits fed.

There's hope in a brand new life,
a lamb, a colt, a calf.
There's hope in the "Lamb of God"
who died on our behalf.

There's hope that "Peace on Earth"
throughout the world will ring
If we will set our hopes on Him,
the Prince of Peace, our King.

Julia Pratt, Dec 2020 I wrote this for
"Light the World" 2020

Seeing God's Plan

It's easy enough
To look back at the stuff
That regretfully one has done.
Remembering the wrong
When one wasn't strong—
Just looking for frolic and fun.

One then must repent
With stalwart intent
And live a much better way.
But memories creep up
And it's hard to stop
The habits of yesterday.

A person who looks
In scriptural books
And studies the words so true—
That someone who prays
Discovers new ways
Of seeing God's plan in view.

Julia Edwards Pratt

Repentance

When we do wrong, we can still sing the song

Of hope and redeeming love.

We all make mistakes, but we can erase,

For Christ was sent down from above.

All of us sin because we're human

And not 'cause we're basically bad.

He changes our heart and gives a fresh start,

Replacing the sad with a glad.

Jesus was sent so we could repent

And seek for his help every day.

So try and do right, and search for the light,

But know that you'll go astray.

Remember to turn and let your heart yearn

To be a lamb in his fold.

He loves you so much; He's willing to touch

And bless and mold and hold.

His love is sure; His motives are pure.

His promises are all true.

He paid the price. He is the Christ.

His Atonement is waiting for you.

Julia Edwards Pratt 2019

HELP ME TO SEE
Julia Edwards Pratt

Sometimes I look up and see
Cloud formations floating free.
Lambs and lions morph and change;
Shapes and patterns rearrange.
Then pondering scientifically,
"Is that a Cirrus cloud I see?"
"Cumulus, Altostratus?"
"I wonder what's the weather status?"
And then at times when I look up,
Shooting sunbeams shake me up.
Frothy clouds become my leaven.
All I see is Father's Heaven.
I try to penetrate the blue
And see beyond the earthly view.

Sometimes I look down by chance
And pass a waif without a glance.
Sidewalk cracks and a littered street
Just blend in with the shoeless feet.
At times I see the poor and judge,
Ignoring Spirit's gentle nudge.
"Is he in filth of his own making?"
"Or is he very good at faking?"
Sometimes my heart will see it right;
The beggar sits in a glow of light.
Life's been hard and fortune missed her;
I see her clearly as my sister.
A smile I give so she knows I care,
A coin and, mostly, a silent prayer.

Sometimes life is going great!
"Wow, am I lucky! How do I rate?"
"Coincidentally things are good!"
"My Karma's working as it should."
And sometimes I take all the credit.
Puff up and blindly say "I did it!"

But sometimes blessings are so apparent,
I remember they come from a loving Parent.
The breadth of grace is not by chance,
But gifts well timed from a Father´s glance,
"Tender mercies" tailor-made for me.
I'm humbled, loved and grateful to see.

When life is hard, and woes persist,
Sometimes I want to escape, resist.
"It's not fair!" be sad, pout, cry,
Impatiently sulk and keep asking "why?"
It's then I need to remember the "plan"!
There's Someone to help when life hits the fan.
When fate deals out its very worst—
That´s when I should put God first.
Reach upward, kneel down, cry unto the Lord,
Share deepest concerns; He hears every word.

"Lord, help me to see
Thy hand in creation.
Help me to see
Each human relation.
Help me to see
Each blessing and gift.
Help me to see
And reach for Thy lift.

Help me to see, how much I need Thee."

By Julia Edwards Pratt
(This was written during our mission to Mexico 2015-2017)

"More Used Would I Be"
Julia Edwards Pratt

"Can I be first?"
"Please pick me!"
"Am I the favorite?"
"I'm eager and free!"

Hearts want to help,
But a common urge
Clouds the offering
With a selfish surge.

The "natural man"[1]
Needs recognition,
Accolades
And high position.

The world teaches
Losing and winning,
Competing, comparing,
Jousting and sinning.

"Who is the greatest?"[2]
Has a familiar ring.
"Can I please sit on the
right hand of things?"[3]

The Savior taught:
Become His child,[4]
To lead is to serve,[5]
Be meek and mild.[6]

The desire to serve
Laced with ambition
Taints the service
And needs contrition.

"MORE fit for the Kingdom"[7]
"More Savior, like Thee"[8]
Precedes the prayer
"MORE used would I be."[9]

1 Mosiah 3:19
2 Matt. 18:1
3 Mark 10:37-40
4 Matt. 18:4
5 Mark 10:44
6 "Jesus Once was a Little Child" Primary Hymn
7 "More Holiness Give Me" Hymn 131
8 *Ibid.*
9 *Ibid.*

OH, HOW LOVELY WAS THE MORNING!
By Julia Edwards Pratt

How lovely was the morning
When the tomb was cold and bare.
A heavy heart came searching,[1]
But hope was in the air.
The law was perfectly fulfilled[2]
And promises were kept.
The risen Lord arose and rescued
All of "them that slept."[3]

How lovely was the morning
When the grove was green and fair.
An eager heart came searching
For answers to his prayer.
The risen Lord descended
With the Father of us all.
This initial vision launched
The prophet's sacred call.[4]

How lovely was the morning
In my bedroom as a youth.
I knelt in prayer for answers,
Like Joseph, seeking truth.
No vision, nor a voice from God,
I felt His presence there.
His light descended on my mind.
My soul filled with His care.

How lovely will the morning be
When all the world will learn,
The Restoration is complete[5]
And Jesus has returned.[6]
Joseph and all prophets then
Will join the heavenly throng.
And we can gather, praise and sing[7]
This old familiar song...

"Oh, how lovely was the morning..." (hymn #26)

1.John 20:11-16 2. Alma 34:13 3.1 Cor. 15:20 4. JSH 1:14-20
5. Acts 3:19-21 6. . Acts 1:11 7. Psalms 138:5
Julia Edwards Pratt
(Easter and the 200th anniversary of the First Vision 2020)

"Find Joy in the Journey"

"Find joy in the journey," our prophet declared, (1)
Though I feel burdened and worried with care.
Should I do what I want? Eat what I crave?
Escape into movies—watch _them_ misbehave?
Can I shop 'til I drop? Buy a grownup toy?
Will that make me happy? Will that bring me joy?

Before I can "find," a search is required,
And scriptures are where these truths are acquired.

"If ye keep my commandments, ye...abide in my love." (2)
There's nothing more joyful on earth or above.
But it's easy to say and harder to try.
If I'm not feeling joy, I should ask the Lord, "Why?" (3)
The Spirit will answer. I may need to repent. (4)
Change can be hard, but it's effort well spent.
If I humbly obey, I'll spiritually grow.
And the joy that I'm seeking will then overflow. (5)

"Find joy and rejoicing in posterity." (6)
Pour my heart and my soul into family.
I'll cultivate love and abandon all strife
To "love joyfully" as a husband and wife. (7)
Children need love when they are young—
Prayers and hugs and work and fun. (8)
With all the awards and applause one achieves,
No joy is greater than a child who believes. (9)
To ancestors who were brave and true,
I'll find joy in finding and serving them too. (10)

Be "joyful in my house of prayer." (11)
In the temple, I'll always find joy there.
I'll go as often as I can,
Keep my covenants and live the Plan.

If I'm feeling dread or done or down,
Acts of service can turn things around.
When I'm serving the "one," I'm serving the Lord, (12)
And feelings of joy are a priceless reward.
If I labor to serve and share and preach
The gospel, and it just happens to reach
The heart of a soul (he repents from sin),
How great shall be my joy with him! (13)

"Men are that they might have joy," (14)
And women too and each girl and boy.
And the most thrilling and joyful thing to know
Is that Jesus came to serve and to show
Me His Light, His Life, His Truth and His Way, (15)
And He's coming again on the very last day. (16)
Faith in Christ makes my joy complete, (17)
Makes my burdens light, makes the bitterness sweet. (18)
He's my Hope, my Lord, my Savior, a Friend (19)
Who'll help me through each dip and bend
Of a joy-filled journey, to a joy without end. (20)

Scriptures on Joy
1. Ensign Nov '08 p84
2. John 15:10-11
3. D&C 136:29
4. Alma 22:15-1617.
5. Gal 5:22
6. Ensign Nov '85 p31
7. Eccl 9:9
8. Family Proclamation
9. 3 John 1:4
10. Mal 4:6
11. Isaiah 56:7
12. Mosiah 2:27
13. D&C 18:15
14. 2 Nephi 2:25-26
15. John 8:12, 14:6
16. Job 19:25
17. D&C 101:36
18. Psalms 55:22
19. D&C 84:77
20. 1 Thes. 5:16

Written for the Lewisville Texas Stake "Poetry Collection"
January 2009

Thoughts on the Corona Virus...

THE CORONAVIRUS BLUES

I look down at my toes,
Worn-out polish—three months old.
Blue-footed boobie blue,
Masked by my shoes,
From another time and place.

When Wuhan was vaguely in the news,
We were traveling carefree in Peru—
Lima, Pucusana.
Last day, we want a
Pedicure for a change of pace.

Mother, daughter sharing an hour
Easily forgotten except for the color
—Our matching blue—
We had no clue
The avalanche of change we'd face.

Global death, Covid-19
Shortages, restrictions, quarantine
Denial and fear
Longing to be near
Held hostage by the virus chase.

They say our world can't recover—

Germophobia, social distancing from each other

An economic shame

With political blame

And all in a hording/vaccine race.

So, I look at my blue toes—

What's left of what seems long ago.

I will not remove it.

I hope it will prove that

There's hope for a future embrace.

By Julia Edwards Pratt (2020)

Masks

There's a question to ask
When you put on a mask
"Why am I covering my face?"
The reasons are many
For masks are a plenty
And used by the whole human race.

From the ancient Shaman
To a Halloween goblin
And to Doctors and nurses too.
Use a scarf or a veil,
A helmet of mail
They all will obscure you from view.

And then there's the kind
Produced in the mind
They make an effective disguise
Emotions rage while
You paste on a smile
But it's hard to hide truth in your eyes.

Am I full of fears?
Or hiding my tears?
Or trying to frighten another?
Am I full of compassion,
Ignoring the fashion
And wearing the mask to save others?

Next time you cover
Just think and discover
"what is this mask really for?"
Pretending or hiding
Protecting or guiding
Make sure that your motives are pure.

If your mask is physical
Or if it's invisible
You know when you've put it on.
Examine your reason
And pray for the season
When masks can all be gone.

Julia Edwards Pratt
Thinking about Covid (2020)

Please-

Let strife cease.
Let love increase.
Let its power release
Our worried hearts,
Our broken parts,
Our failed starts.
Let's strive for peace.
He is peace.
The Prince of Peace.

Julia Edwards Pratt
#Lighttheworld2020

Made in the USA
Middletown, DE
12 July 2021

44012459R00060